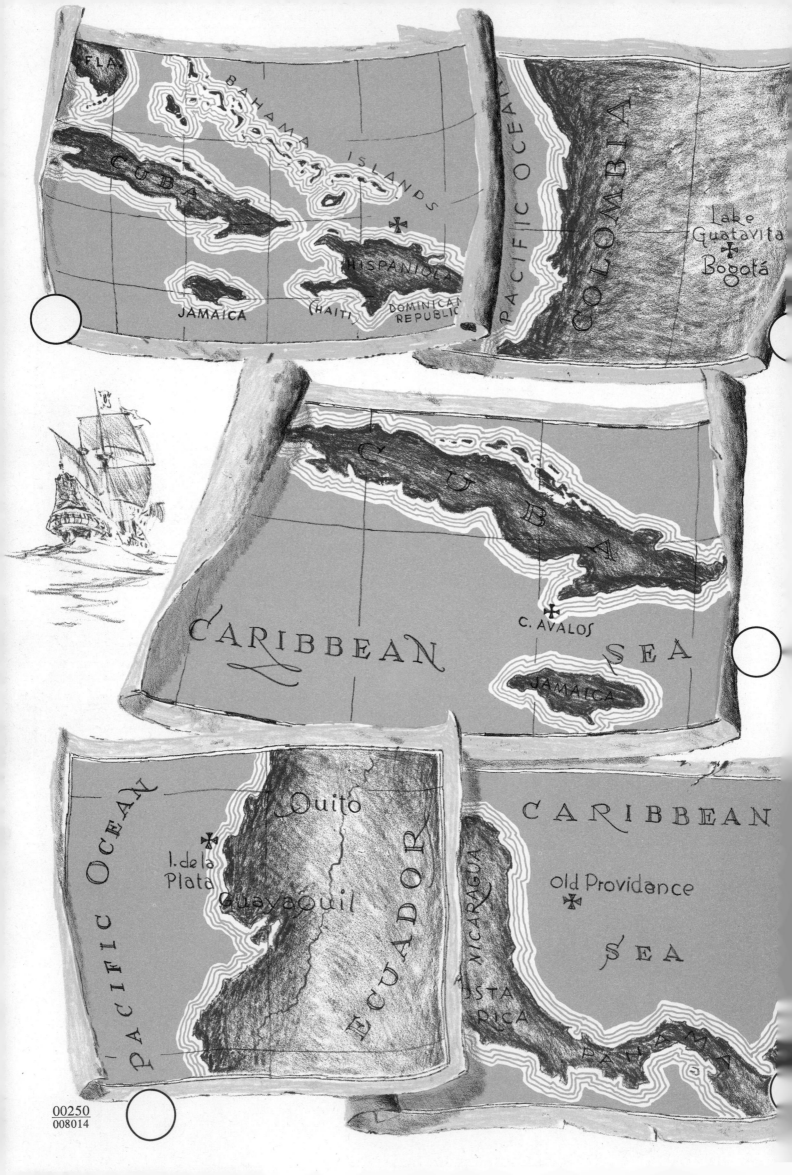

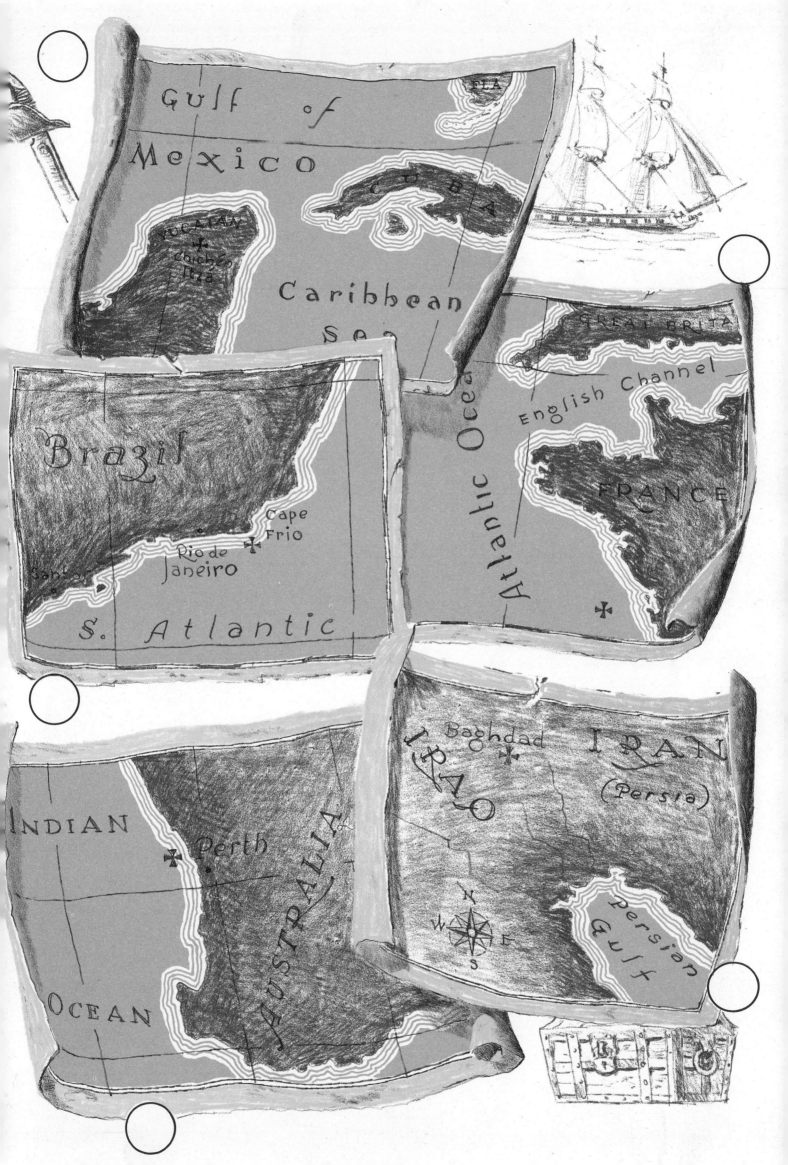

exploring for lost treasure

exploring for
lost treasure

BY NORA B. STIRLING

ILLUSTRATED BY H. B. VESTAL

GARDEN CITY BOOKS, GARDEN CITY, NEW YORK

LIBRARY OF CONGRESS CATALOG CARD NUMBER 60-8305

COPYRIGHT © 1960 BY NORA B. STIRLING

PRINTED IN THE UNITED STATES OF AMERICA

FIRST EDITION

contents

the first treasure hunter

For thousands of years gold and silver have been things men have worked for, fought for, died for. And since they loved them so much, nothing would have delighted them more than to turn treasure hunter and dig up great piles of gold coins buried in the earth or drag up riches from the bottom of the sea. Yet until quite recently no one had ever done so. The reason is simple—there were no lost treasures to hunt for. Indeed, there were hardly any treasures at all.

Until the fifteenth century, when Columbus discovered the new lands of America, the whole of Europe possessed so little gold and silver that if all of it had been lumped together and then divided out evenly each person would have had only about twenty-five cents' worth. And even this was more than they did have, because the kings and nobles had seized most of it. There was a small amount of copper, made up into pennies and other coins, but this, too, was scarce enough, and most people had no money at all. They got the things they needed by swapping with each other, one man doing another man's wood chopping, for instance, in exchange for his new calf. This was called barter, and it was the way people like you and me lived.

6

Then, in 1493, Columbus returned from America. He told the Spaniards about the unbelievably rich lands he had found, and at once a wave of other men rushed over there too, coming back with treasures to make the eyes pop—emeralds the length of your finger, silver melted down into slabs twenty feet long, gold nuggets as big as cauliflowers. Within a few years there was twenty or thirty times as much gold and silver in Europe as had ever been seen there before, and even the poor could have a little. As for the kings and nobles, the warriors and adventurers, they became wealthy beyond even their own past dreams.

Of course, whatever is found can be lost again. And since these vast riches were found in the New World and had to be taken back to the Old in ships a certain amount of it was bound to be lost on the way, either to pirates and highwaymen, or to the storms and rocks of the sea. In the two or three hundred years following Columbus' time enormous fleets laden with treasure regularly made the perilous crossing, but before they could hit the open ocean there were three thousand islands and hidden pointed rocks in the Caribbean Sea to pass, and many a rich ship lost her life upon one of them.

So, for the first time, there were great treasures lying in the sea, lost, ownerless, and waiting for someone to come and pick them up.

In 1643 nearly an entire fleet of such ships went down near the Bahama Islands. The combined cargoes were said to be worth almost fifty million dollars, of which the flagship carried the greatest part, and word spread up and down the North American coast even as far as the Massachusetts Colony.

A young New England sea captain decided to go after the fortune in the flagship. He had little money and no equipment, however, and since the Bahamas and everything in their vicinity were owned by England he had to secure permission from King Charles. So young William Phips left his wife, Mary, his twenty older brothers and his five younger sisters, and sailed away to London.

After a time he met the youthful Duke of Albermarle. Much taken with the idea of a treasure-hunting expedition, the Duke secured a license from the King and with some friends formed a company to back the sea captain. They bought him a couple of ships, the *James and Mary* and the *Henry,* and at last Phips was on his way.

But he had only the vaguest directions for finding the wreck, knowing simply that it had sunk near some hidden rocks that were part of a certain reef. And, being no diver himself, he was entirely dependent on four Indians who were expert divers and were to share in whatever treasure they brought up.

Arriving at the reef known as the Ambrosia Bank, the divers got to work. With no equipment other than a rope around the waist with a knife stuck through it, they grasped a heavy stone in the left hand and dived overboard. Forty, fifty, sixty feet the weight of the stone dragged them down, and on reaching bottom they dropped it and darted about through the branching coral and seaweeds searching for the ship. For days they worked unsuccessfully, and were about to give up. Then it happened that the diver Franko, who fortunately was a man with an eye for beauty, saw a branch of red coral waving about like a flower. He swam over to break it off. But the coral was growing on something much more exciting.

He was back at the surface in a moment, his eyes popping. "A gun!" he gasped. "I've found a gun!"

Immediately another diver went down and broke off another lump of coral. This was long and oblong and clumsy, and when he brought it up and hit it with a metal rake it fell apart, showing white inside—solid

silver. They had arrived over the exact spot where the treasure lay.

In the years since the flagship sank, the wood had rotted away and the gold and silver had spilled out into the sand, to be overgrown and hidden by coral and seaweed. But now they knew where to look.

One after another the divers went to the bottom, grasping the stone and chewing a bit of oily sponge to check the impulse to breathe. For a minute and a half they struggled with a lump of coral and then, jerking at the rope at their waist, were dragged up again with their load. Twenty such dives an hour they made, working eight hours a day every day (except Sunday, for William Phips was an earnest Puritan). The treasure came up in many forms, bars as well as pieces of eight, dishes, buttons, ornaments; there were gold ingots, and jewels, and some very fine guns. After two months the ship was loaded to the gunwales, bursting with her riches, and the end was not in sight.

But the ship was destitute of something else—food. Of course they could return to a nearby port and buy more, but Phips knew that the moment his men hit land some one of them was bound to talk, to brag about how rich they all were, and then every pirate on the high seas would be after them. So, leaving the wreck with vast sums in it still untouched, he took the *James and Mary* and the *Henry* straight home to England without touching port anywhere. They were half starved when they arrived, but the welcome they received was worth the suffering.

Phips was at once the idol of London, being knighted by the King and made High Sheriff of New England. It is true that the King and his high-born friends took most of the treasure, of which Sir William Phips received only sixteen thousand of the three hundred thousand pounds. But since this would be equal to several million dollars today, William Phips, the twenty-first son of a New England farmer, did not do too badly.

Indeed, this first known treasure hunter still ranks as one of the greatest of them all. And considering he used that most primitive of instruments, man's naked body, his achievement is still one of the most remarkable. In the coming chapters you will see how other men have used other means of recovering treasure, some even simpler than Phips's and some very complicated. But all the methods, you will notice, have one thing in common—whether they required no more than a man's body or many machines and gadgets, every one depended on that most wonderful instrument of all, the human mind.

El Dorado's billions

You remember that although the continent of Europe had had very little gold and silver until Columbus' time the countries he discovered were very rich in them. All along the west coast of South America and up into the Andes there was so much the people hardly knew what to do with it all. Many peoples, such as the Peruvians, did not use it for money. (Indeed, they had no money of any sort. Their ruler, the Inca, owned everything in the kingdom, every stick and stone and blade of grass, and there was nothing for anyone else to buy or sell. So they had no use for money.) But everyone liked the appearance of these shiny metals and valued them as ornaments.

Now you have often heard the words *El Dorado*. They are generally supposed to mean some fairy-tale kind of country, fabulously rich and beautiful. Actually El Dorado was a *man*; the words are Spanish for "The Golden Man," and the place where he lived was called the Land of El Dorado, which is how the words got their mistaken meaning.

11

Santa Fe de Bogotá, a city high in the Andes, was the capital of this place, and on top of one of the mountain peaks nearby was a lake about half a mile across. This lake had originally been the crater of a volcano, but after the eruptions ceased the cavity had gradually filled up with melted snow running down from the encircling rim. The Chibchas, the people who inhabited the region, worshiped this Lake Guatavita because they believed that in its depths lived a powerful goddess, Cacica, and her daughter. A temple on its brink contained life-size statues of them in pure gold, and once each year an elaborate ceremony was performed in their honor.

Two cords were stretched at right angles across the lake, and at the exact center where they met, priests and the king, standing on a raft surrounded by musicians and singers chanting hymns, threw overboard offerings of gold and emeralds. This king, who had previously been anointed with a sticky, sweet-smelling oil and then covered with gold dust until he was literally a golden man, then dived into the water to purify himself. Naturally all the gold dust washed off and sank to the bottom. And so after centuries of these ceremonies you can imagine how much gold and gems had collected in that one spot.

In the early sixteenth century the Spanish conquerors appeared on the shores of South America. The riches they had been finding everywhere were driving them nearly mad with excitement, and they stopped at nothing to get as much as they could as fast as they could, stealing and murdering and forcing millions of Indians, as they called the natives, into slavery. The Indians, naturally, tried to save what valuables they could, sealing them in caves, burying them in the earth, throwing them into the water. And so by 1550, when the Spaniards got as far as Lake Guatavita, millions more had been thrown in on top of The Golden Man's sacrificial offerings. Some authorities say there was as much as five *billion* dollars' worth altogether.

The Chibcha chief, Simijaca, threw in the life-size statues. A Spanish captain, Quesada, hearing about it, was so furious he had the chief roasted alive, and then turned his mind to getting the statues out. He tried to drain the water out of the lake, but as fast as his slaves pumped it out the springs from the surrounding mountainsides filled it up again, and he finally had to give up.

This was the first of many such attempts. In 1580, Antonio de Sepulveda, a merchant of Santa Fe, secured permission from Philip of Spain, who owned all these lands, to search for the treasure. The King stipulated that everything found was to go to him, but when Antonio had drained the lake dry and got out the treasure he should have a share.

It was quite a tricky job. Since the lake sat like a bowl of water atop a cone of volcanic rock, he planned to cut through the rim of the bowl, thus letting out the water and exposing the treasure at its bottom. He set hundreds of Chibcha slaves to digging, and they did finally cut away a gap in the side of the mountain. The water poured through and the lake went down several feet. Very much excited, Antonio grubbed about in the exposed mudbanks and found some small gold figures: an alligator, thirteen frogs, and three monkeys. Then he came upon a high priest's miter and, glory of glories, an emerald as big as an egg. Now he was really on his way. Bursting with pride, he sent them all back to the King of Spain, according to his contract.

All this had taken much time and money, of course; his funds by now were running out. But he expected that when the treasure was sold the King would send him his share and this would be plenty to go on with. And the articles did indeed bring a great price, nearly a quarter of

13

a million dollars for the gold figures and seventy thousand for the emerald. But the King reminded Antonio of a certain clause in the contract—he was to receive his share *after the lake was drained dry*. Was the lake dry? No? Then Antonio could wait.

Soon afterwards Antonio woke one morning to find that the cutaway sides of the gap had fallen in and the lake was filling up again. This, on top of the stinginess of the King, was too much for the harried Santa Fe merchant. His treasure hunt came to an end and the lake was left to itself for many years.

But five billion dollars' worth of anything is unlikely to be neglected too long, and there were many other unsuccessful attempts. Then, only sixty or seventy years ago, a modern engineering company with plenty of money got to work. They, too, hoped to drain the lake dry, but they found that, though it was shallow on the edges, in the middle, where El Dorado had thrown his offerings, it was very deep. However, after thirteen years of persistent effort they succeeded; no one in three hundred years had ever got all the water out, but they did. And then imagine their dismay, for at the bottom they found not masses of gold and statues and gems but mud, twenty-five feet of soft, sticky mud.

In some climates this might not have been so bad, but Lake Guatavita lies right on the equator. Once the water was removed, the tropical sun, burning down fiercely from directly overhead, in no time had baked the mud as hard as cement. All the treasures of the Chibchas were baked right in with it, like pebbles in a concrete sidewalk.

At that point the engineers gave up. And it is my guess that until someone invents a way to drain the lake and at the same time keep the sun from shining on it the little gold animals and the priest's miter and the magnificent emerald will be all that the world will see of that five-billion-dollar hoard.

Drake's forty-five tons of silver

There have been many people who have hunted treasure in the last four hundred years, but very few who did it against their will. However, in the case of Drake's forty-five tons of silver not only did the finder try to avoid finding it, but the original owner deliberately threw it away. This is how that happened.

One of the great heroes of England in the sixteenth century was Francis Drake. In those days people didn't think pirates were so bad—if they were on your side, anyway—and Drake robbed only the ships of England's long-time enemy, the King of Spain.

Drake's great feat was to sail his little *Golden Hind* all the way around the world—the second man in history ever to do so. It was a terrible, wonderful journey that lasted from 1577 to 1580 and was made without maps or charts most of the way.

Now as you know, Spain had already got to South America and her explorers were annually sending home a fleet of ships filled with the fabulous riches of Peru. So when Drake reached the west coast he began the most terrific, wholesale piracy you ever heard of. He slipped up on ships and seized them with grappling irons; sometimes he boarded them and cut their moorings, so they were blown out to sea; sometimes he took the captured ships along with him, entertaining their captains at dinner with music and games. (The one thing he never did was kill or maim his victims, and if he took their ship he provided for their safety in some other way.) Many Spanish warships set out in pursuit of him, but his little *Golden Hind* skipped ahead of them all.

All this time he had been collecting the Spaniards' loot. His ship's hold was jammed with it, chests cluttered up the decks. And under this extraordinary weight the vessel was almost sinking. Planning as he was to go home via the stormy Pacific, he realized his ship was too heavy for safety and he had to do something drastic.

What he did was to heave forty-five tons of silver overboard into the water near a little offshore island. And ever since, that spot has been called the Island of Silver—Isla de la Plata, in Spanish. So that's how the silver was deliberately thrown away.

Now, about how somebody later found it against his own will. Almost exactly 350 years later a little man with many college degrees in the fascinating science of mineralogy found himself on this same South American coast. Thaddeus Wilkie had been sent there by an American mining company to look for new mines, but the time was 1932, during the depression, and suddenly the company went broke. He had to get home any way he could, and he hitchhiked up the coast on a dirty old tug with a queer-looking captain and an equally queer crew of five.

As they passed Isla de la Plata, Wilkie made the mistake of letting out that he had studied the records and knew approximately where Drake had dumped his silver. The six thugs were terribly excited; they knew that since the ocean was filled with sharks no diver had ever tried to get it up, and so it must still be there—somewhere. "If you'll show us the exact spot, we'll give you half of everything we find," said Captain Harrow.

16

They fitted out the wheezy old tug with a barge and a dredge that looked like a clamshell. This was to be dropped to the sea bottom and bring up a load of sand containing, they hoped, silver pieces of eight. It was worked with a couple of metal ropes and was the one tool they needed for the job. So out they went to the deserted little island, and after several days the clamshell bucket brought up a huge mouthful of sand, different from those before. In it were sixty-six pieces of eight. Now not only Wilkie but everyone else knew exactly where the treasure lay.

Suddenly everything changed for Wilkie. Though Harrow had been all smiles before, and had faithfully promised him half the proceeds, now he announced that Wilkie was to get only a sixth, like everyone else. And when the little scientist protested he saw that Harrow's hands were playing with a knife on the table. He also remembered uncomfortably that everything he ate was cooked by one of the crew. His life was at their mercy.

At this point he decided to get out, though the silver was coming up richly in every bucketful. But that proved not so easy. What they were doing, it turned out, was highly illegal: the laws of Ecuador and Isla de la Plata required all treasure hunters to get permission from the government and then to give up a large share of what they found. But Harrow and the others had no intention of giving up anything. And they didn't intend Wilkie to go ashore either, for fear he would tell the police. So he found himself thoroughly trapped.

To make things even less comfortable, he realized that now they knew where the silver was he was just in the way and they would like nothing better than to split up his share among them. Indeed, one of the deck hands "accidentally" tripped him up and nearly threw him overboard. And when he looked in his suitcase for his revolver he found it had been

18

stolen. Like it or not, as long as the dredging went on he went on with it.

All he wanted was for the dredging to stop, the whole job to be over, so he could get out safely with his skin. So he put his scientist's brain to work. The line that worked the bucket was made up of many tiny wires. He knew that if only two or three were broken the raw ends would eventually catch in the working and halt the whole operation. So with his heart in his throat he slipped out to the barge during his solitary midnight watch and filed through a few of the dredge's wires. Then he put back his file and waited for developments.

Next day the line ran through perfectly a few times. Then it caught. The thugs examined it and fell to swearing, for their line was ruined and suddenly the whole treasure hunt was finished. They dared not go ashore and buy another line because the authorities would guess what they were up to, and so they had to sail away and leave the rest of the silver lying there. As far as anyone knows, it has remained untouched since.

Wilkie was in luck, in that no one suspected his hand in the accident. The crew simply put him off down the coast, dropping his sixth share off with him in the belief that if he had some himself he would be less likely to tell on the others. But before they sailed away Harrow looked at him long and hard.

"Remember," he said, "if you ever tell anybody about the last two weeks, we'll find you and kill you, if it takes twenty years." Wilkie knew it was true.

So there was the little man, left standing on a lonely beach with a great pile of blackened silver coins. He dared not turn them in to the government for fear of Harrow's vengeance. He could not use them for money, for they were hundreds of years old and good only to put in museums. There was nothing to do but melt them down.

For weeks and weeks he lived in a deserted hut on the beach, each day making a little fire, melting the silver over it in an iron pot, letting it cool, and selling the plain cake of metal at forty-five cents an ounce. It brought thirty-two thousand dollars all told, and at last he returned to America, a much richer man than when he left.

But he never dared tell of his adventure, and the author learned the details only after promising to disguise his identity. So the name Thaddeus Wilkie isn't his real one. But the adventure is, the adventure of the man who found, against his will, a fortune another man had tossed away.

19

the cave on the deserted island

The curious thing about lost treasures is that they can be found so many different ways. Most successful salvages have taken months, even years. Most, too, have cost a lot of effort and money. But occasionally all rules are broken and someone finds a tremendous fortune without any trouble at all, literally stumbling onto wealth. This is one of those cases.

Two hundred years ago, you remember, all ships were sailing ships. In 1733 the brig *Mary* set out from Bristol, England, to one of England's colonies, Honduras. She carried a cargo of lumber, tools, food, and livestock, and on board were young Edward Seaward and his wife, Eliza, and their spaniel, Fidele. By the time they were on the last part of their journey, from Jamaica to Honduras, they were impatient to reach land and start building a home.

A few hours out of Jamaica the wind died. Then, about midnight, it came up again with a roar, getting stronger and stormier, until at noon next day the sky was soot-black, with a queer green light around the edge.

"We're in for a hurricane," said the sailors in dread. And sure enough, while the whistling wind laid the ship over on her side and the waves piled up white onto her decks, there came a crackle of lightning and a gunshot of thunder, and the skies opened like a bucket overturned.

The terrified Eliza stayed down in the cabin out of the sailors' way while Edward tried to help on deck. But as the ship rushed on before the gale and three sailors were washed overboard the lookout gave a horrified cry:

"Breakers! Land ahead!" Now they knew they were going to be wrecked.

Edward rushed down to his wife, while the sailors started launching a lifeboat. But the door locked behind him, and when he and Eliza finally reached deck the boat was gone and they were the only two living souls on a doomed ship.

Then occurred one of those strange miracles that do happen occasionally. The ship didn't sink. It ran onto a sandy bar and stuck, keeling far over but at least safe, and when dawn came they saw that they were near the shore of a small island. There was no sign of the lifeboat; everyone in it must have drowned, and they two were alone on a deserted island.

Now began a strange life, something like that of Robinson Crusoe. Their first meal consisted of drowned hen boiled in sea water over a fire started with the lens of the ship's spyglass, but they gradually learned how to make themselves fairly comfortable with the supplies they found in the hold. Edward brought up some lumber and built a cabin, and Eliza started a garden.

But the climate was very hot, and the food went bad rapidly. So when Edward, out hunting with Fidele, came onto a cave near the beach and found it many degrees cooler inside he decided to use it as a kind of refrigerator.

One day, carrying some supplies to the farther end, he saw something lying on the floor of the cave. When he examined it he nearly dropped with amazement for, of all things, it was a belt. A man's leather belt! And they had thought they were the first people ever to step onto this island.

What they could not know was that this island, called Old Providence, had one of the bloodiest histories of any place of its size on earth. Here, between Mexico and South America, where the Spanish galleons had

21

passed carrying home their fabulous hoards, a colony of pirates had made their home. A kingdom it had been, indeed, ruled over for long by Sir Henry Morgan, often called the greatest pirate in history. Certainly he was one of the richest and most merciless, for Morgan not only robbed the ships of strangers, he robbed his own friends, and at one time made off with a fortune his men had won for him, hiding it no one ever knew where.

After Morgan's death the pirates left the island and it was gradually forgotten, the trees and the grass growing up and covering any signs of former life. So it was not surprising that Edward and Eliza supposed they were the first ever to go there, and you can imagine how curious they were about the owner of that belt.

Their food cave was rocky inside, and one day when Edward shot a giant lizard and wanted to hang it up out of the way of ants he sharpened a short peg and drove it between two of the rocks in the wall. A funny thing happened—instead of the usual dead sound, his hammer made a strange hollow noise. He hit again; no doubt about it—hollow. For the first time he noticed that the rocks were set in a funny regular way, like bricks in a wall. Very excited, he stuck a chisel between two of them and jimmied one out. A few more followed, and peering through the hole, he saw another cave inside.

While Eliza held a candle, he made the hole large enough to climb through. And there on the sandy floor, ranged as neatly as bottles on a shelf, were two rows of canvas bags, and behind them a chest.

When they slit open one of the bags, it appeared, in the dim light, to

contain silver coins. This was exciting enough thirty nine bags of silver pieces of eight!—but when they took one to the sunlight it shone big and round and yellow. A gold Spanish doubloon worth fifteen or twenty times as much. And besides all this the chest held jewelry, sword hilts, gold tissue, church objects of all sorts. They were incredibly, uncountably rich. But what could they do with this wealth on a deserted island? They decided to put it back in the cave and wait for a ship to come by.

All these months they had been watching for a sail. One ship had passed without seeing the flag they waved, but now, after nearly a year, they looked once more and this time saw a boat approaching. Not a ship to carry them home, unfortunately, but a canoe filled with five Negroes who had been shipwrecked some miles offshore. They had managed to paddle to safety, and now Edward and Eliza gladly made them welcome.

So began a little colony. The men were expert workmen and their wives could cook and sew, and everything was very pleasant. Finally Edward's and Eliza's prayers were answered—a real ship was sighted far off on the horizon, and when they fired a gun it turned and came inshore.

So at last their deserted-island adventure came to an end. After freeing the slaves and giving them money to start life over Edward and Eliza took their amazing fortune home to England and lived happily for many years.

But one question always burned within them, waiting to be answered —who had originally owned their wonderful treasure? If they had ever heard of the pirate Sir Henry Morgan, perhaps they might have guessed.

the mystery of the two cannons

To be a good treasure hunter you need several things—a good clue, of course, comes first. Persistence and maybe some strong muscles for digging or diving—they are good too. But nothing quite takes the place of a brain. And this was proved in the case of the two-cannon mystery.

As we've seen before, the Caribbean Sea is filled with small islands, many of them, like Old Providence, hide-outs for pirates who used to wait for ships sailing the trade routes and rush out and hold them up. Directly beside the route from Jamaica to Cuba lay another such island, Cayo Avalos, too small to be found on most maps but highly thought of years ago by various pirates.

Later, of course, pirates went out of business and just ordinary people came to these islands. A man named Brown lived on Cayo Avalos about fifty years ago. Brown had come across a map, a real pirate's map, he was sure, which told where a treasure was hidden. There were a number of clues, or markers, described in it, but when he looked for the first two he was very disappointed. It called for two big trees, but there was not a single big tree anywhere around, and he thought he had been fooled.

24

Then he spoke to an old lady who had lived there all her life, and she said yes, two big trees had once stood right near his house, but they had been blown down in a hurricane and later chopped up for firewood. After this he felt considerably better.

He looked around some more. The next clue was two cannons lying under water. And sure enough, when the tide went all the way out, there on the uncovered beach were two cannons lying half buried in the sand. This was certainly getting interesting.

The best thing yet was the way the cannons were lying—several feet apart, but with the muzzles turned towards each other to form a sort of arrowhead, an arrow pointing towards an interesting-looking large flat rock onshore.

Running to the rock, which he had passed thousands of times in his life, he saw what he had never seen before (which shows he wasn't very observant), some numbers scratched on its surface. Even more exciting, there was a face looking in the direction of his own house, which stood beside a small lake.

He had no idea what the numbers meant, and he was even more puzzled by something else. His house hadn't been there when any pirates were around.

But the lake had. Suddenly he cried, "I have it!"

Immediately he started draining the lake. He figured that this was what the face was looking at, and that the treasure chest must be sunk in it. He pumped and pumped, but no matter how fast he drew the water out it ran in at just the same rate—which he might have expected, because it was so near the sea the water couldn't help seeping in. He never got to the bottom of the lake, and finally he gave up, a disappointed man.

During the years that followed, he and an old friend used to go out occasionally at low tide and sit astride those puzzling cannons. They would look this way and that, wondering, wondering what the map had meant and where in the world the treasure could possibly be. Then he died, and in the 1926 hurricane his house was blown down, and that, it seemed, was the last of the story.

But here's where that little extra something comes in, that brain. For there was another man in the vicinity, let's call him Jones (I'm not allowed to tell his real name because, like the original of Thaddeus Wilkie, he doesn't want it known). Jones knew about Brown's futile hunt and about the lake and the cannons and the marks on the rocks. But he didn't waste his time pumping the ocean out of the lake. He sat down quietly and *thought*.

If, he said to himself, Brown's map really was a pirate's map, the question was, *what* pirate? Obvious answer: one who was known to come to these islands, for not all of them did. So a smart man would find out all he could about the men who worked this vicinity.

26   Carefully Jones studied the pirates' histories. He learned the habits of the famous ones, and then he became particularly interested in Jean Lafitte, for a very special reason.

Lafitte was originally a respectable merchant in the West Indies, but

after his beautiful wife had been killed and he had been robbed by
Spanish pirates he swore to get vengeance. With his brother Pierre he
recruited a crowd of cutthroats and outfitted a ship, and within a year
they had seized a dozen Spanish vessels, killing everyone, stealing all
valuables, and then sinking the ships. They prospered enormously: a
thousand of them ruled an island near New Orleans like a private kingdom, and they became rich by smuggling their loot into the city and
selling it at auction. Occasionally some purchaser would recognize a
jewel or a silver dish that had belonged to a friend now mysteriously disappeared, but there was no positive proof against them, and for several
years the Lafittes went their way unchecked.

Until 1803, Louisiana was not United States soil, but then the Louisiana Purchase took place and the new Governor Claiborne determined to wipe out this pirate kingdom. But Lafitte was so rich and powerful he defied all his efforts: when Claiborne advertised a reward of five hundred dollars for his arrest, he turned around and offered fifteen hundred for Claiborne's. He thought he could get away with anything.

For a while it seemed he was right, for Claiborne had bigger things to worry about—the British Navy, which was approaching to attack. But now Lafitte and his rough, reckless men grew suddenly patriotic and threw themselves furiously against the British, winning quite a name for themselves. So here were the city's enemies suddenly becoming its heroes.

But, as usual in the long run, law and order took over. Louisiana became uncomfortable for the pirates and the Lafittes were driven westward to Texas. There they again became rich and powerful, but there again the law followed. Most of their men were executed, and the brothers disappeared into Mexico. It is known that Pierre was buried in Yucatán, but no one is quite sure how or where Jean spent the last years of his life.

All this Jones learned. But it was none of these facts that interested him most. He had picked up somewhere one small bit of information, and on that he acted. Waiting until the tide was well out, he walked out to the half-buried cannons. Brown and his friend had sat here often and dreamed of a fortune to come. They had seen that the muzzles were stopped with what might have been cement, but that fact had made no impression on them.

Jones was different. He had taken note of that cement. And now with a chisel and hammer he chopped away at it until it fell out in small chunks. And what he found was exactly what he expected, for he had learned that Jean Lafitte had a habit of hiding gold and jewels in empty cannon barrels, sealing them with cement, and dropping them into shallow water until he could come back for them.

Jones was delighted, of course, but not surprised. Nor was he surprised that the other clues, the carving on the rock and arrowhead position of the cannons, meant nothing. False clues were often inserted into a pirate map lest it get into the wrong hands. So, as we said before, a clue is a good starting place, and persistence and muscle are good too. But the thing that really pays off is a brain.

28

the well of sacrifice

The Chibchas who worshiped the goddess at the bottom of Lake Guatavita were not the only strange and fascinating people the early conquerors found when they followed Columbus across the ocean. There were as many different countries and races in America as there are in Europe now, and each had its own customs, worshiped its own gods, and most of them in time disappeared from the earth, killed off by some other invading race. Many left no traces except remains of buildings, clay dishes, perhaps jewelry—things that do not rot or crumble away. And since that time many men have spent their lives trying to find these remains in order to learn what the people who made them were like.

Young Edward Herbert Thompson was one such man. He had read a book written by a Spanish archbishop three hundred years before, describing a country called Maya, in Yucatán. These Mayans were in many ways quite like the Chibchas, although they had lived too far away to have ever known them, and young Thompson, spurred on by curiosity, had to find out if the things that archbishop had written were true.

He got himself appointed consul in Yucatán, the youngest in the American service, and as soon as he arrived went to see Chichén Itzá, the capital city of the ancient Mayans. He helped dig out the ruins of the magnificent buildings, he found the remains of a tremendous temple, and pushing through the jungle, he looked for and found the strangest of all the things the old Spaniard had written about, the Sacred Well of Sacrifice. When he looked down its steep sides, a shiver ran along his spine.

It wasn't the appearance of the well that made him shudder. The well itself was just a lake about a hundred feet across, with seventy feet of rocky sides down to the water's surface, dark green and utterly still. It was what had happened there that was so terrible.

The Mayans feared their gods very much, as the Chibchas did. And because in this hot climate rain was very important the god who controlled the rain, who could send it or withhold it according to his mood, was very much to be feared. This Noh-Och-Yum-Chac was supposed to live at the bottom of the Sacred Well, and whenever there was a drought, which suggested he was angry with the people, the Mayans came here to sacrifice to him and beg him to relent.

For hundreds of years, whenever the Rain God was angry, these sacrifices took place, and were always conducted in the same manner. A search was made for the most beautiful young girl in the entire country. She was to be the bride of the Rain God. She was taken to the temple dressed in the finest garments, while the high priest, wearing a huge headdress of plumes, dedicated her to her future husband, and so convinced was she that she was indeed going to marry a god that she actually rejoiced in her fate. A procession of kings, nobles, warriors, and priests accompanied her along a roadway lined with statues to a spot overlooking the well of sacrifice. There large round balls of incense were lighted, and while drums beat and priests chanted two men lifted her and threw her far out into the lake. Down she dropped, her white garments mirrored in the still water, and then broke the surface with a splash and disappeared forever. After her were thrown many objects of gold and jade, gifts for the god and his beautiful bride. This, the Mayans hoped, would bring them the rain they needed.

Such was the archbishop's story, and when young Thompson looked at the water's quiet surface seventy-odd years ago he resolved to go down and search for proof of it.

He went about it methodically. By dropping a weight on a line he measured the well's depth—seventy-five feet—and decided it would require skilled divers to explore its bottom. So he went all the way to

Boston to take a course in deep-sea diving. This was long before the invention of aqua lungs had made skin diving possible, and anyway, no skin diver could have worked for hours that deep in such darkness. What he studied was the standard diving technique.

For many centuries men had been trying to stay under water with the aid of various contraptions—hoods with tubes to the surface, mostly—but they could never get down more than a few feet because of something called *atmospheric pressure*. At sea level air weighs about 14.7 pounds to the square inch and presses up and out as well as down, with equal force, which is why we don't feel its weight. The air inside the lungs presses outward too, supporting the ribs against the inward pressure from the outside, and it is the perfect balance of the two pressures that saves the lungs from being crushed.

Water, too, has weight, which increases with every foot of depth. So you can see that when a diver goes down he has not only the weight of the air above water level pressing in on him, but all that added water weight as well. This doesn't hurt parts of his body like his hand or head, which aren't hollow, but his lungs, which are, suffer badly. They contain the ordinary air he brought down with him from the surface, and since this air hasn't enough pressure to withstand that of both water *and* air, if the man went down very far his lungs would be crushed in and his ribs broken.

Over the centuries many devices were tried, air bags, tubes, helmets, complete diving suits, but still the men couldn't breathe. Then someone tried using *compressed* air, sent down through a pump. A completely watertight but loose-fitting coverall was worn and into this was pumped air with sufficient pressure to equalize that of the water plus air outside, and at last the divers could go down as deep as they wanted.

Having perfected this technique, Thompson came back to Yucatán with a diver's helmet and suit, and equipment to make a dredge. To learn where the young girls' bodies would have fallen he threw down logs about the same size, and then he and his thirty Indian helpers let down the bucket scoop to clear away dead tree trunks and such trash. For days the scoop brought up vile-smelling muck filled with decayed branches and rocks and the bones of animals. Then, as it went deeper, two strange things appeared, round white balls, like ostrich eggs. At sight of them Thompson stiffened, peered closer, and then gave a shout.

32

These balls were the incense the priests had used in their ceremonies.

From that day on many remarkable things came up—ancient weapons, a rubber snake a thousand years old that writhed like a living creature, images of ancient gods, dishes, more incense. And then—the Indians screamed and ran away when he lifted it out of the mud—the skull of a girl about fifteen or sixteen. Thompson looked at it long, in silent awe. The archbishop had been right then: this was the place of human sacrifice, and into these dark green waters must have dropped many other white-robed girls, brides of the Rain God Noh-Och-Yum-Chac.

Altogether they found more than ninety. Young Thompson hoped they had all really believed they were going to be brides of a great god, for then at least they would have died happily.

After a while the dredge stopped bringing up anything but mud, so now it was time to go down in person. This was what he had gone to Boston for. Setting two men to work the compressed-air pump, he donned his diving suit and prepared to make the first dive. The Indians, who were puzzled by the whole operation, shook their heads at the idea of a man's going down into those haunted black depths. They came over, each one, and shook hands and bade him good-by sorrowfully.

Down, down he went. At first the light was yellow, then green, blue, purple, and finally before he hit mud he was in utter blackness. With bare hands he felt about; twigs and stones came to his fingers, and then a strangely shaped thing he could not recognize by touch. He put it into his pouch and went on searching. At the end of two hours he gave his lifeline the four jerks that said to his helpers "Bring me up," and they received him joyfully, as if he were back from the grave.

He himself could not help feeling a little pride, for working seventy feet under water in pitch-blackness had been a test of his nerve.

The moment his helmet was lifted off he looked at the things he had found. There were tiny statues and rings and bells of gold, copper bells, and flat sheets of gold with pictures hammered into them. And—a mystery no one has ever solved—a strange little animal carved from pure jade, mystifying because jade like that is not native to Yucatán, and how these people came by something usually found in China has never been figured out.

During the following weeks Thompson went to the bottom time after time, and his collection of golden objects grew, all gifts of the Mayans to Noh-Och-Yum-Chac and his bride. More of that extraordinary jade turned up. And when he returned to civilization and revealed his discovery experts hailed it as one of the two most important of the twentieth century, not so much because of the value of the gold and jade as because of what it told them about the Mayan people and their strange and awful well of human sacrifice.

the Quail and the *Egypt*

The Quail's salvage of the *Egypt's* gold is remarkable for two reasons —it was one of the most successful salvage jobs ever attempted, and it was one everybody had said was impossible.

The *Egypt,* a British liner, collided with another ship and sank off the coast of France in 1922, with five million dollars in gold and coins in her hold. The ocean was four hundred feet deep here; nothing had ever been recovered from water even half that deep, and so Lloyd's of London, with whom the cargo was insured, paid the owners in full immediately. There was not a chance, not a prayer, of anyone's ever getting it back from *that* depth.

35

Six years later a fat little Italian whose name, Quaglia, meant *quail* and who looked just like that strutting little bird, said he would like to try, for a fifty-fifty split of the proceeds. Lloyd's agreed, since it didn't cost them anything, and the Quail got to work.

At least that's what he'd *hoped* to do—get to work. But he found that everyone who had been there when the ship sank and was perfectly sure he knew just where she lay—well, each of them had a different idea. The ocean is wide and formless, and even with instruments calculations are hard to make. Besides, after six years memories get vague. So the Quail first had to *find* his ship, and it seemed she could be anywhere within a forty-square-mile area.

Starting out with two small salvage vessels, the *Artiglio* and the *Rostro*, he rigged up a *sweep*. Riding half a mile apart, the two ships held suspended between them a huge chain with which they swept the ocean like a child dragging a skipping rope along the ground; the object was to catch anything (a ship, say) that stuck up in its path.

Back and forth they rode endlessly, back and forth and always a little westward, like a man plowing a field. Storms held them up; accidents killed eleven of their number; Quaglia, who had to pay for the ships and the men and the equipment out of his own pocket, was running out of money. For two solid years they swept for the *Egypt*, and then finally, at a point embarrassingly near where they had first started looking, their line caught on something and at last the *Egypt* was found. Now they could begin the actual work.

The reason Quaglia, of all the salvage experts in the world, dared to undertake this job was that he had perfected a device to take a man deeper than any diver had ever gone before. Of course a diver *could* get down four hundred feet in an ordinary rubberized canvas suit like Edward Thompson's, but if he did that old demon atmospheric pressure messed things up.

Perhaps you have heard of the bends, a disease that used to (and still does occasionally) attack divers on their return from the depths, sometimes killing them, often paralyzing them, and always causing acute agony. While the diver is below, inhaling the compressed air that is being pumped down into his helmet and suit, the extra nitrogen in the air is being forced into his blood and tissues. Since nitrogen causes carbonation, he is thus being turned into a sort of bottle of soda pop, which is held *in* by the ocean's pressure as the soda pop is held in by the glass bottle. When he comes up and the outside pressure is relieved, the stored-up gases expand and fizz exactly as the bubbles in the drinking glass do. This fizzing is the bends, and it can attack the heart, the spinal cord, or the limbs. Anywhere it goes, it is terrible.

Fifty or sixty years ago a great scientist, J. S. Haldane, discovered that the way to counteract the bends was by timing the dives: since it took so long for the body to absorb so much nitrogen, and so long for it to throw it off again, just keep the diver down only so long and bring him up only so fast. This is called natural decompression, and practiced according to Haldane's careful schedules, it has saved thousands of men from suffering and death.

The only trouble is that the deeper a man goes the longer he must take coming up—maybe as long as five hours—and the waste of time means it has never paid to attempt anything below 130 feet in an ordinary suit. And the *Egypt* lay at four hundred.

But the Quail had developed a way of getting around this difficulty. Until now the fearful weight of the ocean was held off the man by the loose-fitting suit which was filled with compressed air and thus formed a kind of protective shell around him. Instead Quaglia built a shell of *metal* to hold it off. This eliminated the need for compressed air. And this in turn meant no more decompression, no more long hours coming up; best of all, no more bends.

The shell Quaglia built for his divers was something on the order of a telephone booth suspended on a cable. There was a phone, canisters of oxygen to keep the air fresh, a seat, and windows all around, and the man inside could direct the operation of the huge instruments let down from the surface.

The plan was to cut through the steel plates of the ship and lift out the gold with huge tongs. But the *Egypt* was sitting upright on the bottom, the gold was stored deep under five decks, and the shell and tools, being suspended from the *Artiglio* above, could work only up and down —that is, neither tool nor man could attack the ship sideways, which meant that they must cut a hole straight down through the five decks. Dynamite would do it, but each charge had to be let down from the surface, the men above directed by the man down in the shell, and then the grab was let down to lift out the cut-off pieces. It was so dark the divers could not see more than ten or fifteen feet, and the currents pulled the shell and the dynamite charge this way and that, while the *Artiglio* above rose and fell on the waves. Sometimes it took a whole working day to get one charge set in place.

Months went by; a year. All over Europe the public was reading about this ridiculous engineering attempt, discussing it, wondering if Quaglia could really pull it off. They didn't realize the difficulties and how bad the weather was (there was one month when the crew got only five working days). All they knew was that Quaglia had taken two years even to find the ship and now he seemed to be making a complete fool of himself. All Quaglia knew was that he was dead-broke and the banks didn't want to lend any more money.

38

But persistence paid off. The blasting and cutting and lifting went on, and at last the bullion room itself was laid open. Then the rush was on: in three days they lifted out nearly a million dollars, and papers all over the world were hailing Quaglia as an engineering genius.

When the job was finished three years later, 98 per cent of the gold had been recovered and the Quail was many times a millionaire. But perhaps the greatest pleasure he got was in saying "I told you so" to a skeptical world. They had said it couldn't be done and he had done it.

Captain Dickinson's bell

You have already learned about some of the methods people employ to go down under water. There's still another way, and if you want to understand this one get yourself a large cork, a stub of candle, and a drinking glass. Set the candle on the cork, light it, and set the cork floating on a bowl of water. Then turn the glass upside down over the lighted candle and press down. (If your cork is too small and your candle too large, so that it overturns, run a large nail up through the cork into the candle, and its weight will hold the cork upright.) Now when you press down you'll see that the air will stay in the glass and the candle will remain alight no matter how far down it goes. The air inside is pressing against the water and keeping it out.

This is the principle of the diving bell. Inside one of these a man can go to the ocean's bottom and stay safe and dry—except for his feet, of course, which he has to stand on. In the old days he could stay down only as long as the oxygen lasted, but then compressed air pumps were invented, and after that there was almost no time limit.

It was with a diving bell that Captain Thomas Dickinson performed his miracle of treasure recovery for an ungrateful boss.

The *Thetis,* a British man-o'-war, left Rio de Janeiro for London on December 4, 1830, carrying £160,000, or about eight hundred thousand dollars. Two days later, on a black and stormy night, she was driven onto a rocky island off Cape Frio and, pounded against the jagged cliffs, began to break up. Some of the men managed to scramble onto a point

40

of rock jutting out overhead, but more fell into the water, while still others were crushed against the cliff. Before the ship went down, a wind drove her along the coast into a sheltered inlet, and it was there she sank.

Hearing the news in Rio de Janeiro, other British sea captains gave up the *Thetis* and her treasure for lost. But Captain Thomas Dickinson of the sloop *Lightning* differed. He was familiar with Cape Frio and he knew where the wreck lay, and finally he approached the Admiral.

"I believe, sir," he said, "that the *Thetis'* gold and silver can be salvaged."

The Admiral stared at him as if he were half-witted. "Nonsense," he puffed, and walked away.

But Captain Dickinson kept on dreaming about his scheme. Once more he approached the Admiral, this time with drawings and calculations, and his commander in chief, though hating to admit he could be wrong, had to let him try. But it was plain that, having once said the captain couldn't do it, he devoutly hoped he wouldn't. That's the way stubborn people are.

But Captain Dickinson could be stubborn too, and though his friends begged him to give up the idea he went on slaving night and day over his plans. Since at the spot where the wreck lay the currents were too fierce to permit divers to go down, he needed a diving bell. But there wasn't such a thing in the country. So he made a funny-looking bell out of two

old water tanks, with a compressed-air pump to go with it, and after six weeks the *Lightning,* whose crew by this time had got into the spirit of the thing, made off for Cape Frio. The Admiral watched glumly; he didn't even say good-by.

When they arrived, Captain Dickinson wondered if he had been a fool. What he found was an island with steep, rocky cliffs two hundred feet high; four hundred feet across a gorge the mainland's cliffs were equally high and steep. Between rushed the fifty-foot waters in which the *Thetis* lay. To get at it they had to lower the bell from something directly overhead. But there wasn't anything, so Captain Dickinson's task was to make it.

What the Admiral had lacked in enthusiasm was made up by the crew, who loved and admired their captain. A mile down the coast they gathered timber from the wreckage and made a derrick arm 158 feet long. They towed it to the inlet and hauled it halfway up the cliff, securing it on a platform dug out of the earth. Finally they attached the bell to heavy wire cables, and they were ready to go.

No one knew what would happen, though everyone knew all too well what could. Maybe you noticed when you were experimenting with your candle and glass that if you didn't push down absolutely evenly the air came bursting out and let in water that drowned the flame. Well, Captain Dickinson knew that could happen to his men.

And that's what nearly did, the first time two of them went down. The heavy iron bell had sunk forty-five feet. Captain Dickinson, peering down through the clear water, saw the currents tossing the bell about violently, and all of a sudden the whole thing overturned and the air came bursting out. One man, Dewar, came up with it and reached the surface in safety. The other, Heans, became entangled in a line. Horrified, Dickinson watched him struggling to free himself.

In only the few seconds that his breath lasted, he managed to slip free and, gasping and purple-faced, reached the surface alive. After a couple of minutes he grinned weakly at the other diver.

"Never mind, mate," he said, "this thing hasn't beaten us yet."

42 And it hadn't, although it was two months before anyone knew whether their efforts would pay off. In the meantime the men were suffering tortures. Mosquitoes buzzed around their heads in clouds so thick they could not see through them, and they were forced at times to

bury themselves up to their necks in the sand to escape their bites. Malaria developed, with its high fevers and chills, and various other sicknesses wore them down to skeletons. Food soon became scarce, and from then on they were half starved. But they kept gallantly at the job, mainly because of Captain Dickinson.

At last, on March 27, the pay-off came. Taking down with them a pick and a saw, Heans and Dewar came to rest standing on the wreckage. Blueprints of the *Thetis* had told them where her strong room was situated, and they had gradually worked down through the broken wood of the hulk. This day, as usual, they had taken a flat wooden board which, since there were no telephones, served as a slate. Now they wrote on it, shoved it out from under the lip of the bell, and it floated to the surface.

Dickinson looked at the message: "Lower the bell a foot, we are now over some dollars."

Good news at last! Dickinson's face glowed with delight. And now that things were going well they never stopped night or day, and after five days had brought up $6,326 in coins, 285 pounds of silver bullion, and four pounds of gold. For a month they continued, the treasure totaling now $58,300. Then Dickinson stopped to take thought. He had done this all on his own: the Admiral had blocked him wherever he could, refusing him supplies and enough men, and there was no telling what reports had gone back to London. Perhaps he should send in the results of his work to prove he was succeeding.

This he did, and soon he was glad that he had, for a terrible storm came up which for fourteen hours tore at his beloved derrick until finally it fell from the cliff in a mass of wreckage.

But even then he wasn't beaten. Starting all over, he strung a suspension cable across the gorge from the island to the mainland, and with a new diving bell got to work again.

45

Months passed and the treasure mounted. By March 1 of the next year six hundred thousand dollars had been accumulated and only two hundred thousand remained below. Dickinson felt fine; he even began to dream a little. Surely now the higher-ups in London had heard how hard he had worked; surely now there would be a word of praise, a little pat on the back. . . .

But he forgot the Admiral. On March 6 the British sloop *Algerine*, under Commander the Honorable J. F. F. de Roos, sailed in and dropped anchor. De Roos, looking a little uncomfortable, handed him a letter. Captain Thomas Dickinson, it seemed, was being ordered to resign his charge in favor of Commander the Honorable de Roos. The Commander would finish the job and Dickinson was to go home.

The captain could hardly believe the words on the page. But it was true: the Admiral was having the last word.

Plainly Commander de Roos was embarrassed. And the captain, though hurt and shocked, was still too big to take it out on his brother officer. Instead of quickly salvaging the last of the treasure so De Roos would have nothing to do, he showed him how to use the bell and where to look for the money. Then he sadly sailed away, leaving De Roos to wind up the job and sail home in a blaze of glory.

No one has ever understood the Admiral, except by recognizing that some people are just made that way. But here is the interesting end to the story. I said the Admiral had had the last word. But I was wrong. After all these years Captain Thomas Dickinson's name is respected all over the world and that of the Admiral is hardly known.

the Baghdad junk-dealers

This is a treasure story that is different from the others. Though the treasure is lost, it is not sunk in the ocean or hidden in the ground. And though it is still being hunted, the men who are going after it are not divers or explorers or anyone of that sort. A whole government, a whole country, is on its trail. And it is so great a fortune that few people have ever dreamed of owning so much. The story begins over a hundred and forty years ago.

In Baghdad, which used to be part of the Ottoman Empire and is now the capital of Iraq, there lived two brothers, named Elazar and Shimon Levy. They were exceedingly poor, men who lived by buying up junk nobody else wanted and looking through it for something to sell. And so badly were they doing in Baghdad that in 1814 they went to nearby Persia to try their luck there. And what luck they had!

One day they brought home a cartload of trash collected from all over town and began sorting it out piece by piece. The most unpromising thing in the pile was an old clay kettle. It was filthy and cracked, and they decided there was no point in saving *that* old thing. They tossed it on the scrap heap.

That might have been the end of the story, but their luck was terrific that day—they threw it down with enough force to break the crack wide open, and when it fell apart out poured a perfect shower of jewels, hundreds of the most beautiful diamonds and pearls and rubies and everything else you can imagine.

When the brothers recovered from their shock they quickly hid the jewels and, trembling with excitement, discussed what to do with them. One thing was certain, they couldn't just go out and sell a few rubies and buy themselves clothes and a fine house. Everyone would ask where the rubies had come from, and someone was sure to claim the old kettle. Maybe the Persian Government itself would arrest them and take it away.

The same thing was true of Iraq. The only solution was to go some
place far away, where they weren't known and no one would ask any
questions. The dangers ahead were great, and Elazar, who was married,
didn't dare take along his wife and young son. He didn't even tell them
what he had found—it wasn't the custom for men to discuss their business
affairs with their wives. He just told them to wait there until they heard
from him

He and Shimon hid their jewels among their ragged belongings, and
after a perilous journey through Persia and Iraq, terrified every minute
of being discovered and robbed, they got on a boat bound for London.
Along the journey they sold a few jewels and bought some fine clothes;
they even added a title to their names; and by the time they reached
London, Aga Shimon and Aga Elazar were very elegant men indeed.

After turning the rest of the jewels into cash and investing it in good
safe businesses Aga Elazar sent for his wife and son. This boy's name was
Yair, but he had another name, which he came by in an interesting
fashion: he had been very ill at one time; according to an old Jewish
belief, he was being pursued by the Angel of Death. It was thought that
if another name were added to his own this would throw Death off the
scent, so he became Yair-Refuah, and thus he has been known ever since.

After the two brothers died, the entire huge fortune went to this son of
Elazar. And then Yair-Refuah, who had had a childhood sweetheart back

in Baghdad, wrote the girl's father asking for her hand. Yair-Refuah must have loved her very much, for when her father answered that he wasn't going to send his daughter all that distance alone, and if Yair-Refuah wanted her he must come and get her, the young man sold out his interests in England, put aside some of the cash to take with him, and left the rest deposited in certain English banks. Then, in 1827, he went back to Baghdad and got married.

Very soon the young couple had a son, then another and another and another. At last, about 1833, Yair-Refuah decided to take them all back to England. But before they could leave he fell ill—so ill he was unable to speak. He had never talked about his business to his wife, and his sons were too small for such things, and now it was too late, he could never tell anyone about his fortune in England.

He could still move his hands, however, and he signaled for his family to hand him the family Bible. As he turned its pages, they assumed he was just looking for his favorite passages, and after he died they put all his papers and books away in the attic and forgot about them altogether.

Many years passed; the four sons grew up and they in turn had children. Finally, about 1890, one of Yair-Refuah's grandsons was cleaning up the attic when he found an old trunk full of books and papers. In it was the Bible, falling apart and crumbling along the edges. Turning the pages out of curiosity, he saw some writing. He thought he recognized the Hebrew script and compared it with his grandfather's. Sure enough, it was Yair-Refuah's. Part of the page was missing but the rest contained some words that made his hair stand on end: " . . . two hundred thousand gold pounds at four and a half accumulative interest in ban . . . England . . . I leave my entire fortune to my four sons in equal shares. Accounts number .·. . Yair-Ref . . ." The edge of the page had crumbled away, and part of the signature was gone. Most importantly, the names of the English banks were gone. But it was the will of his grandfather all right, disposing of nearly a million dollars. His grandfather had left England in 1827 and the interest on this million had been piling up ever since. By now it must be an enormous fortune.

This was sixty or seventy years ago. All the children of all the children in the Levy family, back to Elazar and Shimon Levy of Baghdad, saw themselves getting rich. There was just one catch: no one knew what banks in England held the money. And it had been so long ago that the banks themselves didn't know. Somewhere, in some dusty old vault, must be the original papers Yair-Refuah had filled out when he turned the money over, but there were thousands of bank vaults and each one would have to be searched.

Since the discovery of the will over four hundred Levy descendants have been found, most of them Jews living in Israel. If they could find the money, it would be brought back to Israel, which would make not only them but the country they live in very rich, for money invested at 4½ cumulative interest and accumulating thus over a hundred and thirty years becomes a staggering sum.

Several very important lawyers are doing their best to locate the papers, and the state of Israel itself has put up a large sum to have the bank vaults searched. In the meantime all four hundred Levys are keeping their fingers crossed: if those papers of Yair-Refuah ever turn up, they stand to inherit not a penny less than two hundred million dollars. And that is one of the largest treasures you or I have ever heard of.

something better than treasure

Most treasure seekers are men looking for adventure and gold. But a hundred years ago one John Cutler, a diver by trade, found something more valuable than either. His story took place in West Australia, a strange place indeed at that time.

This vast continent had been claimed and opened up by England not long before, and little groups of pioneers were going out and settling on farms. But it was being used for something else than farms. The penal laws of England (and in most other places) were extremely harsh—fifteen years in jail for stealing an oak beam, twenty years for setting fire to two haystacks—with the result that the jails were jammed. But when that enormous stretch of empty land opened up, here was a perfect dumping ground, and thousands of convicts were sent out and turned over to local settlers as slave labor for the duration of their terms.

The cruelties and horrors these men suffered were indescribable. In some places they actually drew lots for the privilege of murdering their keepers, not for revenge but as a means of getting themselves quickly hanged and so put out of their misery.

The eastern part of Australia was the first colonized, and by the time the West was settled the scandals of the convict camps had shocked the authorities into deciding to send out no more prisoners. But later the

52

Western settlers requested free labor too. They stipulated, however, that they would accept no murderers or other hardened criminals, and so that was how John Cutler, a big strapping man of twenty-five who was serving fifteen years for shooting rabbits on an earl's estate, came to land at Perth, West Australia in June, 1850. He had left a young wife and two babies back home, and he was very sad about that, but he was naturally a pleasant sort of fellow, and because the *Scindian's* captain had not starved the convicts or flogged them on the way out, he suggested that all seventy-five send him a letter of thanks.

As was the custom, he was kept in a Perth jail for nine months to see how he behaved, and then, the only diver in the entire colony, was sent to clear the mouth of the Swan River. That, though he didn't know it at the time, was the best bit of luck he ever had.

On Friday the third of September, 1852, he was sitting in his cell reading a Life of Napoleon from the prison library. Outside a storm was howling, the rain crashing on the jail's tin roof, and through the other noises Cutler dimly heard several booms of thunder. Other people heard them too, and said to themselves, "My, what a terrible night!" But the sound they heard wasn't thunder.

Earlier that evening, the captain of the barque *Eglinton,* bringing a group of English settlers and £15,000 in gold, had announced that they would reach port tomorrow. The passengers, despite the storm battering the ship, had organized a birthday party for one of the young ladies, and everyone was very gay and festive.

Suddenly, at 9:45, the lookout shouted, "Breakers ahead!" Before the helmsman could alter his course the ship crashed onto a reef. The waves pushed her right over it, and then over a second, but when she hit the third reef she shuddered and stopped dead, impaled on the jagged rocks with her head up and her stern deep under water.

Panic took hold, but no one dared try to leave the ship in the dark. At daybreak they saw shore not far away, and two boats were let down, which foundered in the heavy surf. A third, however, managed to land and some men immediately started off for Perth, twenty-eight miles away. Miraculously, all on board were brought safely to shore except one very fat lady and the cook, who was drunk and jumped overboard.

The sounds those at Perth had heard were the *Eglinton's* guns being fired for help. But no one had given them a second thought till the survi-

53

vors brought their news, and then a police boat and a detachment of soldiers rushed to rescue the men, the women, and the gold.

In those days £15,000 was about the same value as half a million dollars now. This fortune lay deep in the submerged stern of the ship, which was threatening to break up against the sharp rocks. So John Cutler, who had proved himself as a diver in the Swan River operations, was rushed to the spot to salvage it before it sank.

The compressed air pump was set up on the forward deck and Cutler descended into the strong room. Though the interior was pitch black and he had to work by feel alone, the gold was in square boxes and should be easy to locate. But all he found was stacks of round casks. Then he remembered—there was gunpowder there too, and the gold must be behind that. Tugging and heaving, he dislodged one or two casks. Suddenly a third gave way and the whole pile came down. At the same moment a violent tug on his helmet jerked him off his feet.

Sprawled on the floor, he felt for his lifeline and air hose. The line seemed to be free, but the hose was pinned under the pile of casks. Thus his supply of air was cut off. With what remained in his suit he could live perhaps eight minutes. After that, unless he freed himself, he would suffocate.

54

Desperately he shoved at the casks, breathing heavily under the extra exertion. With each gasp more oxygen was used up and more deadly carbon dioxide exhaled into the helmet. His head began to swim, his consciousness to fade. He knew he could never free himself in time, so with his last strength he drew his knife and cut the hose. At the same moment he gave his lifeline the danger signal, and by the time his helpers had jerked him up his suit was half full of water and he was unconscious. But at least he was alive.

Later, when he had recovered, the captain of police clapped him on the back. "Good man. I'll see you get your V.G. for this." *V.G.* stood for Very Good, two letters sewn on the sleeve of convicts with outstanding records.

That night Cutler had a chance to get something more tangible than letters on his sleeve. A number of fishermen with small boats had been hanging about the wreck watching. Now, in the dark, they approached Cutler and began whispering in his ear. "What is a convict like you co-operating with the police for? What will you get out of it? Why not work with us? You can say the ship's bottom was torn out and the gold has been lost into the ocean—there's no one who can go down to check on what you say. You can pretend to try to find it. And then when they've

55

given up and gone away, you and we can come back and get it. We will split fifty-fifty. You'll be rich." It must have been a temptation.

But Cutler shook his head. "I've got a wife and kids I want to bring out here, and I'm not going to get into trouble." The men swore at him, he swore back, a fight started, and the rest of the camp waked and inquired the cause. Again the police thumped him on the back.

In twenty-one days Cutler brought up the entire £15,000 and turned it over to the authorities. "I'll see you get a reward," the Governor General told him, and wrote to London for permission to give him £200. "That's a huge sum for a convict," he said, and Cutler agreed.

A few days later Cutler sent word to the Governer, "Sir, I am grateful for your offer. But could you keep the two hundred pounds and give me my freedom instead?" The Governor wrote London again, word coming back that the Queen ordered him freed and given the money into the bargain. So now he had a full pardon.

With the £200 he sent for his wife and babies and moved to Broome, where the pearl industry was beginning to boom. He taught his young son to dive, and some years later they found a magnificent pearl worth £10,000, which they invested in real estate, and thus prospered mightily.

Now Cutler's family is one of the most prominent and respected in West Australia . . . and all because John Cutler chose something he thought more valuable than treasure.

56

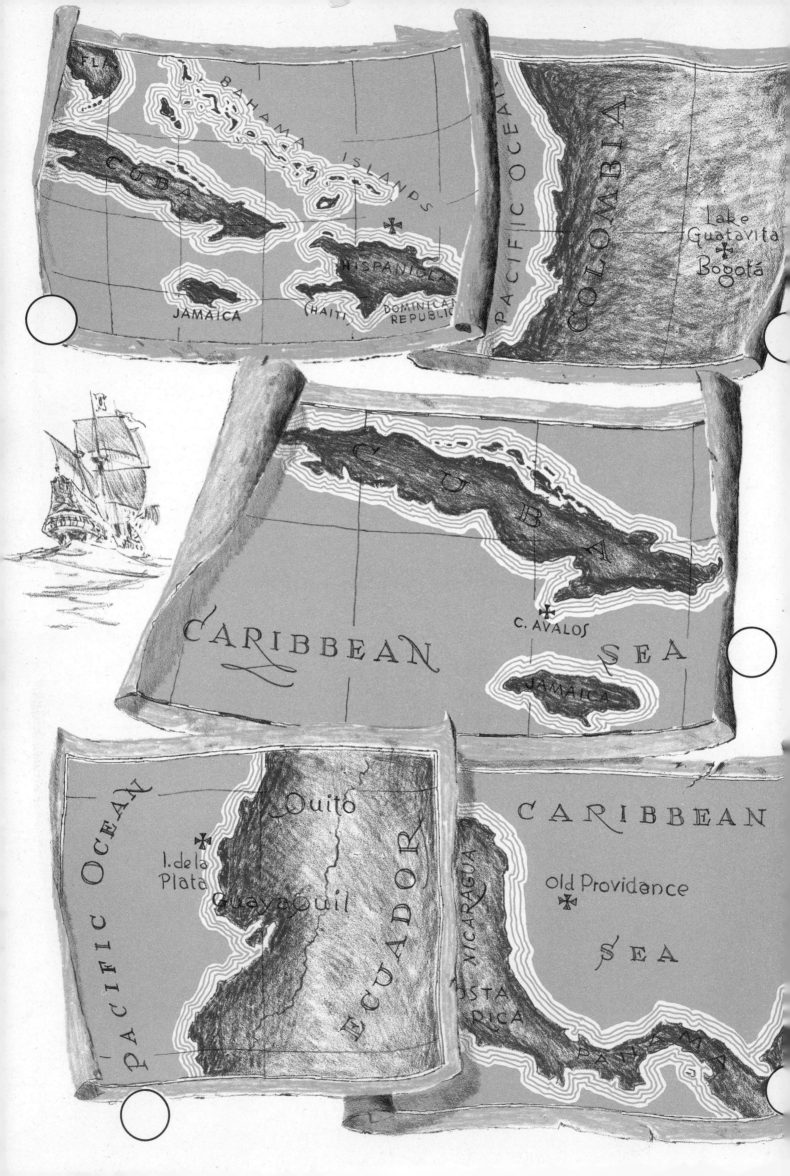

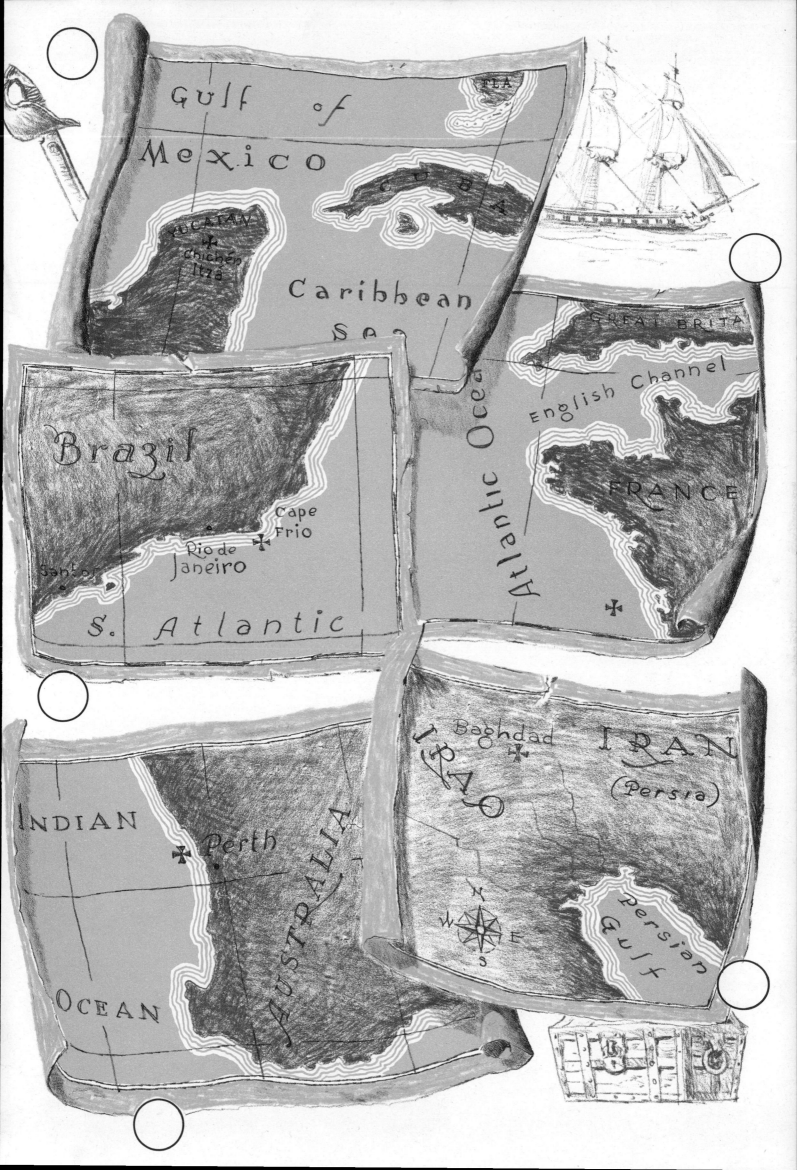